A Selection of Short Poems
by Victor Hugo

ISBN 9780993515118
Bysome Books 2016

Printed in Guernsey by;
www.printedinguernsey.com

Note; Translations from:

The Poetical Works of Victor Hugo
Translated by Various Authors &
Collected by Henry Llewellyn Williams
George Bell & Sons, Covent Garden – 1885

The Distance & the Shadows
Anvil Press Poetry 1981
By Harry Guest (with kind permission)

Gregory Stevens-Cox (with kind permission)

Introduction

Victor Hugo was born on 26th February 1802 in Besancon, France. Hugo showed a precocious talent for writing poetry and in 1820, Louis XVIII awarded him a gift for his Ode *Sur la Mort du Duc de Berry.*

Hugo became caught up in politics during the 1840's and had to flee to exile in Belgium. After being compelled to leave Belgium, he re-established himself and his family in Jersey, but he fell foul of the authorities and decided to move to Guernsey in 1855. After a year, he purchased a house in Hauteville, St. Peter Port. This gave him security – as a house owner he could not be banished for political reasons.

Hugo developed a busy life in Guernsey, rising early and spending his morning writing in his study at the top of Hauteville House.

The years of exile in Guernsey were very fruitful for Hugo, and he completed *Les Misérables, Le Contemplations, La Légende des siécles, and Chansons des rues et des bois,* amongst other works.

Guernsey and the seas around its rugged coast became the setting for *Les Travailleurs de la mer* (Toilers of the Sea), a novel that works on several levels; superficially it is a love story, but it also addresses such diverse themes as nature and the Industrial Revolution.

When the rule of Napoleon came to an end, Hugo returned to France. He visited Guernsey on three subsequent occasions, at least once because he wanted some peace and quiet to write!

Victor Hugo died on 22nd May 1885, millions grieved his death.

Gregory Stevens-Cox

Old Ocean - *(Les Orientales, 1829)*

I stood by the waves, while the stars soared in sight,
Not a cloud specked the sky, not a sail shimmered bright;
Scenes beyond this dim world were revealed to mine eye;
And the woods, and the hills, and all nature around,
Seemed to question with moody, mysterious sound,
The waves and the pure stars on high.
And the clear constellations, that infinite throng,
While thousand rich harmonies swelled in their song,
Replying bowed meekly their diamond-blaze –
And the blue waves, which nothing may bind or arrest,
Chorused forth, as they stooped the white foam of their crest:
'Creator! We bless thee and praise!'

(R.C. Ellwood)

Roses and Butterflies *(Les Chants du Crépuscule, 1835)*

The grave receives us all;
Ye butterflies and roses gay and sweet,
Why do ye linger, say?
Will ye not dwell together as is meet?
Somewhere high in the air
Would thy wing seek a home amid sunny skies
In mead or mossy dell –
If there thy odours longest, sweetest rise.

Have where ye will your dwelling,
Or breath or tint whose praise we sing,
Butterfly shining bright,
Full-blown or bursting rosebud, flower or wing.
Dwell together ye fair,
'Tis a boon to the loveliest given;
Perchance ye then may choose your home
On the earth or in heaven.

(W.C. Westbrook)

More Strong than Time (les Chants du Crépuscule, 1835)

Since I have set my lips to your full cup, my sweet,
Since I my pallid face between your hands have laid,
Since I have known your soul, and all the bloom of it,
And all the perfume rare, now buried in the shade;

Since it was given to me to hear one happy while,
The words wherein your heart spoke all its mysteries,
Since I have seen you weep, and since I have seen you smile,
Your lips upon my lips, and your gaze upon my eyes;

Since I have known upon my forehead glance and gleam,
A ray, a single ray, of your star; veiled always,
Since I have felt the fall upon my lifetime's stream,
Of one rose-petal plucked from the roses of your days;

I now am bold to say to the swift changing hours,
Pass; pass upon your way, for I never grow old.
Flee to the dark abysm with all your fading flowers,
One rose that none may pluck, within my heart I hold.

Your flying wings may smite, but they can never spill
The cup fulfilled of love, from which my lips are wet.
My heart has far more fire than you have frost to chill,
My soul more love than you can make my love forget.

(A. Lang)

Morning *(Les Chants du Crépuscule, 1835)*

Morning glances hither,
Now the shade is past;
Dream and fog fly thither
Where night goes at last;
Open eyes and roses
And the darkness closes;
And the sound that grows is
Nature waking fast.

Murmuring all and singing,
Hark! The news is stirred,
Roof and creepers clinging,
Smoke and nest of bird;
Winds to oak trees bear it,
Streams and fountains hear it,
Every breath and spirit
As a voice is heard.

All takes up its story,
Child resumes his play,
Hearth its ruddy glory,
Lute its lifted lay.
Wild or out of senses,
Through the world immense is
Sound as each commences
Schemes of yesterday.

(W.M. Hardinge)

The Ocean's Song *(Les Châtiments, 1853)*

We walked amongst the ruins famed in story
Of Rozel Tower,
And saw the boundless waters stretch in glory
And heave in power.

O ocean vast! We heard thy song with wonder,
Whilst waves marked time.
'Appear, O Truth!' thou sang'st with tone of thunder,
'And shine sublime!

'the world's enslaved and hunted down by beagles,
To despots sold,
Souls of deep thinkers soar like mighty eagles,
The Right uphold.

'Be born, arise, over earth and wild waves bounding
Peoples and suns!
Let darkness vanish, tocsins be resounding,
And flash, ye guns!

'And you, who love no pomps of fog, or glamour,
Who fear no shocks,
Brave foam and lighting, hurricane and clamour,
Exiles – the rocks!'

(Toru Dutt)

The Seaman's Song *(Les Châtiments, 1853)*

Farewell the strand,
The sails expand
Above!
Farewell the land
We love!
Farewell, old home where apples swing!
Farewell, gay songbirds on the wing!

Farewell riff-raff
Of customs' clerks who laugh
And shout;
'Farewell!' We'll quaff
One bout
To thee, young lass, with kisses sweet!
Farewell, my dear – the ship flies fleet!

The fog shuts out the last fond peep,
As 'neath the prow the cast drops weep.
Farewell, old home, young lass, the bird!
The whistling wind alone is heard;
Farewell! Farewell!

(Toru Dutt)

Oh, Why not be happy?
(Ruy Blas, Act II)

Oh, why not be happy this bright summer day,
'Mid perfume of roses and newly mown hay?
Great nature is smiling, the birds in the air
Sing love-lays together, and all is most fair.
Then why not be happy
This bright summer day,
'Mid perfume of roses
And newly mown hay?

The streamlets they wander through meadows so fleet,
Their music enticing fond lovers to meet;
The violets are blooming and nestling their heads
In richest profusion on moss coated beds.
Then why not be happy
This bright summer day,
When nature is fairest
And all is so gay?

(Leopold Wray)

To My Daughter Adele *(Les Quatre Vents de l'espirit, 1881)*

You slept near me as a baby
fresh and rosy as the Christ-child
in the cradle and your slumber
was so tranquil that you never
heard the bird sing in the shadow
while I breathed the sombre beauty
falling from the vault of heaven
as I though about you.

Listening to the angels flying
overhead I watched you sleeping
and I'd scatter in the silence
jasmine petals on your bed-clothes
keeping guard above your eyelids
closed in sleep and say my prayers
weeping when I thought of all that
waits for us in the night.

One day soon it will be my turn
sleeping on a bed of shadow
in a room so bleak and silent
I shan't hear the bird sing either.
When the night is black around me –
then your tears, your prayer, your flowers
will, my dove, repay my coffin
what I once gave your crib.

4th October 1857

(Harry Guest)

Words Spoken in the Shadows *(Les Contemplations, 1856)*

She'd say, 'The hours go very sweetly by.
'I'm wrong in wanting more, I know.
'You're there. My gaze has never left your eye
'Where I can watch the thoughts that come and go.

'To see you is my joy – though never whole.
'It's still delightful, to be sure.
'My ear's attentive, for I know my role –
'To stop the bores from bursting through the door.

'I sit in my own corner out of sight.
'You are my lion. I'm your dove.
'I hear the papers rustle as you write,
'And stoop to pick up your pen too, my love.

'I have you, to be sure. I see you there.
'Thought is a drug and those who spend
'Their time in dreams forget. I know. But spare
'One thought for me those evenings when you bend

'Over your books and never speak to me.
'Shadows cast on my heart remain,
'My love. For me to see you properly
'You must look at me too, now and then.'

(Harry Guest)

To France *(La Légende des siècles, 1859-83)*

Book!
Go wind-bourne
to France,
where I was born!
Uprooted, root torn,
the tree doth shed
a leaf
quite dead

(Gregory Stevens-Cox)

Shooting Stars *(Les Chansons des Rues et des Bois, 1865)*

See the scintillating shower!
Like a burst from golden mine –
Incandescent coals that pour
From the incense-bowl divine,
And around us dew drops, shaken,
Mirror each a twinkling ray
'Twixt the flowers that awaken
In this glory, great as day.
Mists and fogs all vanish fleetly;
And the birds begin to sing,
Whilst the rain is murmuring sweetly
As if angels echoing.
And, methinks, to show she's grateful
For this seed from heaven come,
Earth is holding up a plateful
Of the birds and buds a bloom!

(Marwood Tucker)

June Nights *(Les Rayons et les Ombres, 1840)*

In Summer, after the day's passed, spread
with flowers, the meadows shed
a fragrance masking the sense. Sleep
becomes transparent and you keep
you eyes closed half aware
of the drifting sounds of summer.

stars are purer now
and the shadows show
themselves less dark. Half-light
is hazed gently across the full height
of the sky. Dawn bides its time seeming
to hover on the horizon all night long.

   28th September 1837

(Harry Guest)

Waiting (Les Orientales, 1829)

Esperaba, esperado.

Squirrel, go and climb the pine,
reach that branch beneath the cloud
thinner than a length of twine.
Stork that each day haunts the proud
steeple, wing towards the keep,
leave your tower for the bell
on the topmost citadel.

Eagle, leave your eyrie, fly
to the age- old mountain peak
where eternal winters lie.
Let the early lark whose beak
scatters song as dawn appears
leave the ground and soaring high
mount the summits of the sky.

From the tree-top, from the spire
On the watch-tower, can you see –
from the mountain, from the air
red with sunshine, can you see
through the haze a tossing plume,
then a smoking horse then
my beloved once again?

   June 1828

(Harry Guest)

The Song of Those Who Go to Sea *(Les Châtiments, 1853)*
(Breton Tune)

Farewell to the land
The waves start to swell
Farewell to the land
Farewell
Blue is the sky and blue is the swell
Farewell

Next to the house the vine grows tall
The flowers show gold above the wall

Goodbye to the land
The wood, field and sky
Goodbye to the land
Goodbye

Goodbye to the girl who wears your ring
The sky is black, the salt winds sting

Farewell to the land
To the girls you knew well
Farewell to the land
Farewell
Blue was the sky and blue the swell
Farewell

Grief for the future dims our eye
The dark sea leads to a darker sky

I'll pray for that land
With all my heart
Loving it well
As I depart
Farewell to the land
Farewell
   At sea, 1 August 1852

(Harry Guest)

'At Dawn Tomorrow.......' (Les Contemplations, 1856)

At dawn, tomorrow, when the landscape's whitening,
I shall set off. You are expecting me.
I'll take the forest road, the upland road.
I can't go on living so far from you.

I'll walk, eyes focused on my thoughts,
the world around unseen, its sounds unheard,
alone, unrecognized, back bent, hands folded,
saddened; for me the day will be as the dark.

I shall not watch the gold as evening falls
nor distant sails downstream towards Harfleur
and on arrival I'll place on your grave
a wreath of holly twined with heather-flowers.

    3rd September, 1847

                (Harry Guest)

A Little Girl.......(Les Contemplations, 1856)

A little girl sees her granny spinning.
She wants a hank of flax for her doll
and bides her time.
There! Granny's nodding off,
so she steals up, pulls
a strand as the bobbin spins,
and triumphant skips away
with some wool dyed saffron-gold –
about as much as a bird would take
building its nest.

    Cauterets, 25 August 1843

                (Harry Guest)

My Two Daughters *(Les Contemplations, 1856)*

Twilight now with cool
shadows falling on the day
as two girls, one a swan,
one a dove, sisters, each
beautiful and both content,
sit on the threshold of the garden
in sweetness, at peace, when
above them white carnations –
their slender stalks set in a marble urn –
are taken by the wind,
lean trembling in the shade,
resembling a flight of butterflies
held there for a moment,
motionless,
living,
in rapture.

    June 1842
                (Harry Guest)

Morning *– Sleeping (The Art of being a Grandfather)*

I hear voices. Gleams of light across my eyelid.
A bell is tolling at St. Peter's church.
Shouts of bathers: "Nearer! Further! No, here!
No, there!" The birds twitter, Jeanne as well.
George calls her. Cock crows. A trowel
Scrapes a roof. Horses pass in the lane.
The swishing of a scythe cutting grass.
Clashes. Confused sounds. Roofers tramp over the house.
Sounds from the harbour. Whistling of hot engines.
Military music coming in snatches.
Uproar on the quay. French voices: "Merci,
Bonjour. Adieu." It must be late, for here
Comes my robin to sing near me.
Din of distant hammers in a smithy.
The water laps. Sound of a steamer puffing.
A fly comes in. The sea's boundless breath.

(Gregory Stevens-Cox)